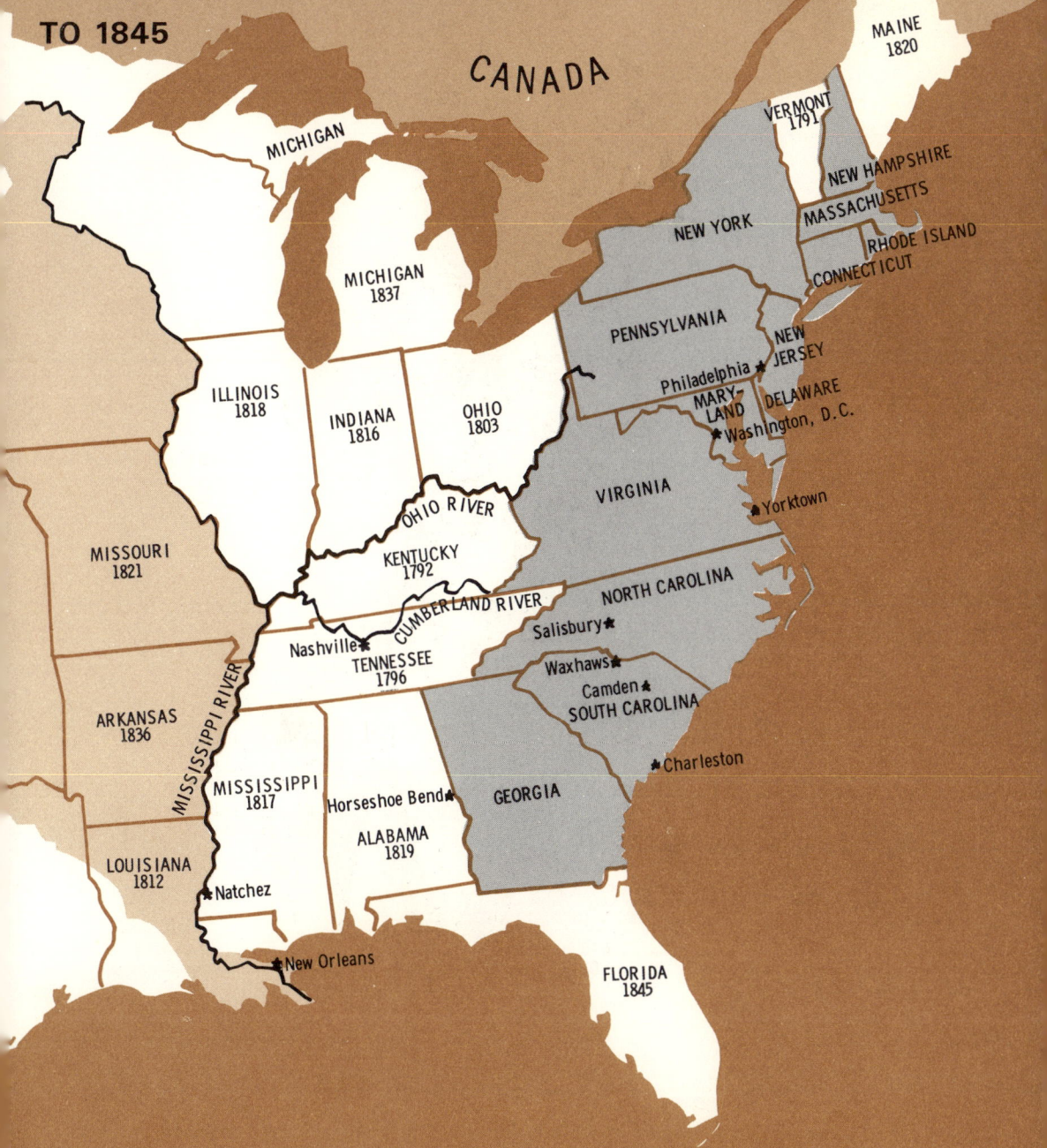

COUNTRY GREW

TO 1845

CANADA

MAINE
1820

MICHIGAN

VERMONT
1791

NEW HAMPSHIRE

MICHIGAN
1837

NEW YORK

MASSACHUSETTS

RHODE ISLAND

CONNECTICUT

ILLINOIS
1818

INDIANA
1816

OHIO
1803

PENNSYLVANIA

NEW
JERSEY

Philadelphia ★

MARY-
LAND

DELAWARE

★ Washington, D.C.

OHIO RIVER

MISSOURI
1821

KENTUCKY
1792

VIRGINIA

★ Yorktown

CUMBERLAND RIVER

NORTH CAROLINA

Nashville ★

TENNESSEE
1796

Salisbury ★

ARKANSAS
1836

Waxhaws ★

Camden ★

SOUTH CAROLINA

MISSISSIPPI RIVER

MISSISSIPPI
1817

Horseshoe Bend ★

GEORGIA

★ Charleston

LOUISIANA
1812

ALABAMA
1819

★ Natchez

★ New Orleans

FLORIDA
1845

Meet

ANDREW JACKSON

By ORMONDE DE KAY, JR.
Illustrated by ISA BARNETT

Step-Up Books — Random House
New York

For Gareth and Charlie

Printed by Rae Publishing Co., Inc., Cedar Grove, New Jersey

Contents

1
MEET ANDREW JACKSON

Andrew Jackson was the seventh President of the United States. He was a great President. And he was a great American soldier.

Before Andrew Jackson was born, his father and mother lived across the sea from America. They lived in Ireland. Ireland was ruled by the King of England, King George III.

Mr. and Mrs. Jackson did not like the way King George ruled Ireland. They decided to go to the English lands in America.

These lands were called colonies. There were 13 colonies in America.

Four of Mrs. Jackson's sisters had already gone to the colonies. They lived in the colony of South Carolina in a little place called the Waxhaws. Mr. and Mrs. Jackson decided to go there, too.

In May, 1765, the Jacksons came to America with their two baby boys, Hugh and Robert. They came to the city of Philadelphia, in the colony of Pennsylvania.

From Philadelphia, the Jacksons started south by wagon. They went through wild, lonely country. They crossed high hills and wide rivers. At last they came to the Waxhaws.

Mr. Jackson bought some land. He cut down trees to clear fields. And he planted corn and wheat.

In 1766 Mrs. Jackson told him she would soon have another baby.

That winter Mr. Jackson was hurt working in the fields. On a snowy day in early March he died.

Mrs. Jackson and her friends put his body on a sled pulled by a mule. They made their way over snow and ice to Waxhaw Church. They buried Mr. Jackson in the cold ground.

Mrs. Jackson went to live near by in the home of one of her sisters. There, before the sun came up on the morning of March 15, 1767, Andrew Jackson was born.

2
THE COLONIES GO TO WAR

Young Andy had light red hair and blue eyes. He was bright and quick. When he was only five, he could read. By the time he was eight, he could read long words. In those days many grownups had never learned to read. Andy often read their letters to them.

Andy went to school at Waxhaw Church. He played with friends in the woods around the Waxhaws. He climbed trees. He went fishing. He hunted deer and bobcats.

Sometimes he watched cockfights. In a cockfight, roosters fight each other with their beaks and claws.

Andy often visited his cousins, the Crawfords. There, he heard angry talk about King George.

The King lived across the sea, in England. Even so, Waxhaws people had to pay him taxes. But they did not see why they should pay. They did not feel English any more. They felt they had become Americans.

Andy learned that many people in the other colonies felt this way, too.

Then Andy heard exciting news. In the Massachusetts colony there had been a battle. Colonists had fought English soldiers.

The 13 American colonies went to war with England. The head of the colonists' army was General George Washington of Virginia.

In June of 1776 more news came. English warships were in the sea off Charleston, the capital of South Carolina. Waxhaws farmers took up their rifles. They elected Robert Crawford to be their captain. And they marched away to Charleston.

In July the men came back. They were very happy. The colonists had driven the English ships away!

3

THE GREAT DECLARATION

In August, 1776, the postman from Charleston brought a newspaper to the Waxhaws. It was a Philadelphia newspaper. Everyone knew that the leaders of the 13 colonies had been meeting in Philadelphia. People in the Waxhaws wanted to know what the newspaper said.

Forty people crowded into Captain Crawford's house. Andy was ready. He opened the newspaper. He began to read in a high, clear voice. The words he read would change the world. These words were called the Declaration of Independence.

The Declaration of Independence had been written and signed by the leaders of America. It said the 13 colonies were free of King George. It said the colonies were states on their own.

The war was not between England and its 13 colonies any more. It was between England and the 13 "United States of America."

In 1778 another country joined the war. It was France. France was on the side of the Americans.

In 1779 the English came back to Charleston. Again men went from the Waxhaws to fight them. Again the Americans won. But many died. One was Andy's brother, Hugh.

Next spring, the English captured Charleston at last. They took 5,400 prisoners. It was the worst defeat of the war for the Americans.

The Americans who got away from Charleston headed for the hills around the Waxhaws.

But English soldiers followed them.

On May 29, 1780, some American soldiers were resting at Waxhaw Creek. All at once, Englishmen on horseback came riding out of the woods. Their swords flashed in the sun. Shouts and moans filled the air.

In a few minutes the Englishmen rode away. One hundred Americans lay dead. Many more were wounded.

Soon wagons full of wounded men rolled up to Waxhaw Church. The men were carried inside. They were laid in rows on the straw-covered floor. Andy's mother washed their wounds and put bandages on them. Andy and Robert helped her.

Andy was only 13, and Robert was 16. But they both wanted to fight the English. They became soldiers. In the first battle the boys were in, the Americans beat the English.

One day in April, 1781, the Jackson boys were at Waxhaw Church when English horsemen rode up. Andy jumped on his horse and dashed away. In a while he found Robert. The boys hid in the woods all night.

Next morning they crept to the house of a Crawford cousin. They thought they were safe. But a man told the English where they were.

The boys were at breakfast when they heard horses. The door flew open. English soldiers stepped in.

4
PRISONERS OF WAR

The English officer in command had mud on his boots. He told Andy to clean off the mud.

Andy said he would not do it.

The officer grew angry. He pulled out his sword. Andy threw his left arm up to protect his eyes.

The sword slashed down. Andy cried out. His hand was cut to the bone. He had a deep cut down the left side of his face.

When the officer found that Andy and Robert were brothers, he kept them apart. He ordered some of his men onto their horses. The English horsemen made Andy walk along a muddy road. They made him walk 40 miles without any food or water.

At the town of Camden, Andy was put in an English prison with some other prisoners of war. Robert was put in the same prison. But he was in another room. Andy did not know his brother was there.

Then a terrible sickness spread through the prison. It was called smallpox. More and more prisoners fell sick. Some died. Before long, Robert was sick with smallpox.

Through a window Andy could see the English camp. One day he saw American soldiers on a nearby hill. Could they capture Camden? Andy kept watching. But a guard nailed a piece of wood across the window.

All night Andy dug away at the wood with a razor. By morning he had made a small hole. He could see through it. He could tell the other prisoners what was going on.

The English attacked. American cannons roared. The English ran.

Andy and the prisoners cheered.

But the English attacked again. The Americans ran. The cannons were quiet. The English had won.

Next day Andy caught smallpox.

That same day his mother came to the prison. She wanted to take her boys home. The head of the prison was a kind man. He let the boys go.

The Jacksons made their way home in a pouring rain. Robert was so sick he had to be held on a horse. Andy walked barefoot beside him.

Two days after they all got home, Robert died. Andy was so sick he did not know what was happening.

For weeks Mrs. Jackson took care of Andy. At last he got better.

But two nephews of Mrs. Jackson were prisoners in Charleston. They were very sick. Mrs. Jackson felt she had to go help them, even if she fell sick, too.

As she said good-by to Andy she tried not to cry. "Andy," she said, "never tell a lie or take what is not your own. Make friends by being honest, and keep them by being steadfast." Then she was gone.

That fall Andy heard great news. General Washington and the French had beaten a huge English army at Yorktown, in Virginia. It might be the end of the war.

But sad news followed. Andy's mother had died in Charleston.

5
CHARLESTON AND SALISBURY

Andrew was alone. But he owned the Jacksons' land. And he did not have to fight any more. The United States had won the war at Yorktown.

When Andrew was 15, one of his grandfathers died in Ireland. The old man left Andrew some money. The money was sent to Charleston. Andrew rode there to get it.

The city seemed very grand after the Waxhaws. On every side stood beautiful old houses with gardens. In the streets, carriages rattled and rolled over the cobblestones.

Andrew soon learned that life in Charleston was not like life in the Waxhaws. Rich men in Charleston owned Negro slaves. The slaves had to work for them. Most slaves were paid no money for their work.

The rich Charlestonians loved to have a good time. Most of all they liked to race their horses. Andrew went to the races. He bet on horse races and cockfights. He lost some money on bets. He spent money on parties and fine clothes. Before long, all his money was gone.

For a while Andrew taught school. Then he moved to Salisbury, in the state of North Carolina. There, he decided to become a lawyer.

He studied laws. But he was still a fun-loving young man. He did not work hard. In those days a man could become a lawyer in just three months. Andrew took three years!

Andrew was 20 when he became a lawyer. He had to decide where to work. In the towns and cities of the East there were many lawyers. But in the land to the west there were very few.

West of Salisbury were mountains. North Carolina stretched on beyond them to the far Mississippi River. Many Americans were going to that wild land to live. Soon there would be work for many lawyers there.

Andrew decided to head west.

6
JACKSON GOES WEST

Andrew Jackson rode west with a band of people who wanted to start new lives in the wilds. Soldiers went with them, for the woods all along the way were full of Indians.

26

These Indians did not want white people in their hunting grounds. They often killed white travelers.

Jackson and the rest were lucky. Indians did not attack them.

The travelers made their way over the mountains. They followed the Cumberland River. And they came to the little town of Nashville.

In Nashville Jackson went to live in the house of a woman named Mrs. Donelson. There he met Mrs. Donelson's daughter Rachel.

Rachel had dark eyes and a sweet smile. She was pretty and kind. Like many women in the West, she smoked a pipe.

Rachel was married. Her husband was Lewis Robards. They had lived in Kentucky, at that time a part of Virginia. Robards was an odd man. He had grown angry with Rachel over nothing, and sent her home.

Then he came after her. He took her back to Kentucky. But Rachel was very unhappy with him. Mrs. Donelson sent Jackson to rescue Rachel from Robards.

Again Robards came after Rachel. But this time she would not go with him. He said it was because she and Jackson were in love.

Jackson was furious. He said he would cut off Robards's ears.

Robards went back to Kentucky.

7
A COTTON PLANTER

More and more people came over the mountains into western North Carolina. They started farms. They planted wheat, corn, and cotton.

Jackson planted cotton. He owned many cotton fields. Men who used him as their lawyer often paid him with land. He owned slaves, too. They worked in his fields.

Jackson made money growing cotton. Cloth-makers in the East needed cotton. They bought it from farmers in the West and South.

Cotton from around Nashville was sent away in boats to be sold. The boats sailed down the Cumberland River, the Ohio River, and the long Mississippi River. At the city of New Orleans the cotton was sold. From New Orleans ships carried it away to the cities of the East.

New Orleans was owned by Spain. All the land from the Mississippi River to the far Rocky Mountains was Spanish. This huge, wild land was called Louisiana.

Jackson went to the Spanish town of Natchez by the Mississippi River. He bought land near Natchez, at a place called Bayou Pierre. He built a house there. He planned a farm.

Then he went back to Nashville.

One day Rachel heard that her husband and some friends were coming to carry her off to Kentucky. Rachel was afraid. She wanted to get away to Natchez. But Indians lived along the way. Would Jackson go with her to keep her safe?

Jackson took Rachel to Natchez. Then he returned to Nashville.

Robards did not come for Rachel after all. But he did send a letter to a friend near Nashville. In the letter he seemed to say clearly that he had divorced Rachel.

Jackson hurried to Natchez to tell Rachel. He said he loved her. And he asked her to marry him.

8
A NEW WIFE
AND A NEW STATE

In August, 1791, Jackson married Rachel near Natchez. They went to Bayou Pierre for their honeymoon.

Across the Mississippi River they saw the woods of Spanish Louisiana rolling westward like a green sea.

After a few weeks at Bayou Pierre, Mr. and Mrs. Andrew Jackson rode back home to Nashville.

Jackson sold his land in the far-off Waxhaws. He bought a house by the Cumberland River. There, he and Rachel lived together.

Two years went by. The Jacksons were busy and happy. Then one day Jackson saw a law paper that upset him. The law paper came from the new state of Kentucky. It was about Lewis Robards. It said Robards had divorced Rachel only a short time before.

So for two years Rachel had been married to two men at once!

Andrew and Rachel were married all over again. Now Rachel was married to only one man, Andrew Jackson.

By 1795 there were 70,000 North Carolinians west of the mountains. With that many people there, this part of the state could be a state on its own. First a constitution or set of laws must be written. Then the men in the United States Congress would have to approve these laws.

Jackson met with other leaders. They wrote a state constitution. And they gave the new state a name. It was Tennessee.

In most states only white men who owned land or paid taxes could vote. But the Tennessee leaders thought poor men should vote, too. Tennessee's constitution said all white men could vote.

The Tennessee constitution was sent to Philadelphia, the capital of the United States. There, the men in Congress argued over it. Some said Tennessee should not let poor men vote. Some said it should. At last the congressmen voted to let Tennessee into the United States.

The new state of Tennessee sent two senators and a representative to Congress in Philadelphia. The representative was Andrew Jackson.

9

A CONGRESSMAN AND JUDGE

In Philadelphia, Jackson and the representatives from other states met in a large meeting hall. There they helped to make new laws.

One day the senators came there, too. They came to hear a great man speak. He was the President of the United States, George Washington.

Washington had been President for eight years. Now he had come to say good-by to the senators and representatives in Congress.

Washington was America's first President. Americans were sad that he was leaving.

America needed a new President. Who would he be? Would he be John Adams of Massachusetts? Or would he be Thomas Jefferson of Virginia?

Jackson was for Thomas Jefferson. He thought Jefferson took the right stand on America's problems.

England and France were at war. England was America's old enemy. France had been America's friend. Jefferson wanted France to win the war. Jackson did, too. But Adams seemed to be for England.

Jackson was for Thomas Jefferson for another reason. Most people in America were farmers, like Jackson. Jefferson wanted to help farmers. But Adams was for businessmen in the big cities of the East and North.

In the election of 1796, Jackson voted for Jefferson. But Jefferson lost. John Adams became President.

Next year Jackson was elected a senator. But he had to give it up. He owed people money. His pay as a senator was not high. He went back to growing and selling cotton. At last he could pay back the money.

Then he was made a state judge. He rode all over Tennessee trying cases. He made friends by being honest. He kept friends by being steadfast. People began to call him the best judge in Tennessee.

In 1800 Jackson again voted for Thomas Jefferson for President. This time Jefferson was elected.

Two years later, Jackson won an election. Soldiers of the Tennessee Army elected him their general.

As a leader in Tennessee, Jackson was interested in Louisiana, to the west. One day he heard France had taken Louisiana away from Spain. Now New Orleans was a French city.

President Jefferson was afraid France might stop Americans from selling their cotton in New Orleans. He asked France to sell the city to the United States.

France sold the city to the United States, and with it, all Louisiana!

Jackson wanted to be governor of Louisiana. He hurried to America's new capital city, Washington. But another man had been picked.

Jackson was still a judge and a general. But he owed money again. He gave up being a judge. He tried to make money in many ways. Often he was away from home.

One day he heard a story. A man named Dickinson was telling it all around. Dickinson said Rachel had known she was married to Robards when she married Jackson.

At once, Jackson dared Dickinson to a duel. In those days men often fought duels to settle arguments. They fought with swords or guns.

10
A DUEL TO THE DEATH

In Tennessee duels were against
the law. So Jackson and Dickinson
rode north to Kentucky.

They took their places in a field,
24 feet apart. Then they raised
their pistols.

Dickinson fired first. His bullet
slammed into Jackson's chest. But
Jackson did not fall down. He fired.
Dickinson fell, with a bullet in his
stomach. That night he died.

Rachel was sad that Jackson had killed a man because of her. But she was glad that he was at home more than he had been. Jackson gave up traveling. He became a full-time cotton planter.

The Jacksons now lived in a large log house near Nashville. It was called the Hermitage. Jackson kept fast horses there. He often raced them against other horses.

In Jackson's fields slaves picked cotton. Some people in the North were saying it was not right to own slaves. But Jackson felt the way most other Southerners did. He felt it was all right to own slaves. He called his slaves his "family."

The Jacksons had no children of their own. But there were children at the Hermitage. They had been born to friends and relatives of the Jacksons. The parents of two had died. And the parents of the other two could not take care of them.

Andrew and Rachel Jackson took the children in. They loved them. They brought them up as their own.

America's government in the city of Washington was far away. But at the Hermitage Jackson kept up with the news. In 1808 James Madison was elected President.

Jackson was not pleased. He was afraid President Madison would be too easy-going with the English in England's war with France.

England needed sailors. English ships often stopped American ships at sea. The English took American sailors onto their ships. And they made them fight the French.

Jackson wanted to make England stop kidnaping Americans. He was ready to fight England. More and more Americans felt the same way.

Jackson and other Americans had another reason for fighting. They wanted more land. They wanted to take Canada from England. And they wanted to take Florida from Spain.

In June of 1812 President James Madison asked Congress to declare war on England. Congress did.

In Nashville General Jackson put on his uniform. He put on his sword. And he got the Tennessee Army ready for war.

Then he sent a letter to President Madison. He said he could take over all of Canada.

All that summer Jackson waited for orders. All that fall he waited. But no orders came.

11
"OLD HICKORY"

At last the governor of Tennessee sent for Jackson. The governor had a letter from the secretary of war in Washington. Tennessee soldiers were needed in New Orleans.

On January 7, 1813, Jackson led
his men to the Cumberland River.
There, boats were waiting. The men
climbed into the boats. On shore,
women and children cheered.

General Jackson started down the
river with his soldiers.

They sailed down the Cumberland, Ohio, and Mississippi Rivers. At Natchez, Jackson got new orders. His men were not needed after all. He was to dismiss them on the spot.

Jackson was angry. His men were hungry. Some were sick. And the way home was over land, through woods and swamps.

Jackson hired wagons to carry the sickest men. He loaned his horses to other sick soldiers.

General Jackson was on foot as he started to lead his soldiers on the long march north.

He joked with his men. He helped them on. He kept them going. They liked him more and more for it.

Once, after Jackson had just gone by, some soldiers talked about him.

"He's tough," said one.

"Tough as hickory," said another, naming the hardest wood he knew.

By the time Jackson's men were in Tennessee they were calling him "Old Hickory." The nickname stuck.

The war was not going well for America. In the South some Creek Indians were fighting for England. They were called Red Sticks.

One day the Red Sticks attacked a fort. They killed hundreds of men, women, and children. A few other people got away. They were hiding.

"By the Eternal," Jackson cried, "these people must be saved!"

12
THE CREEK WAR

To save the Americans and punish the Red Sticks, Jackson rode south at the head of his men.

In their first battle of the Creek War, Jackson's men killed 200 Red Stick warriors. They captured 84 Red Stick women and children.

One prisoner was a boy just three years old. Jackson asked the women about him. They said that the boy's father and mother were dead. There was no one left to look after him.

"Kill him, too," the women said.

Jackson put some brown sugar in water. He gave it to the boy. Then he sent the boy north in care of a soldier. Jackson was going to take the little Indian into his family as his son.

Because of Old Hickory's victory, many Creeks who had been for the English came over to the side of the Americans. To punish them, the Red Sticks attacked one of their villages. There, Jackson attacked the Red Sticks. His men killed 300.

All winter Jackson fought on. In March, 1814, he won a big battle at a place called Horseshoe Bend. The Red Sticks were finished. Their chief came to Jackson and gave up.

Old Hickory was already a general in the Tennessee Army. After he won the Creek War, he was made a general in the United States Army. Then he was sent to New Orleans.

He was worried by the way the war with England was going. The English had set fire to Washington. Across the sea they had beaten the French. More English soldiers were already on their way to America.

Late in 1814 Jackson learned that English soldiers had landed near New Orleans. He had his men build a mud wall along a dry canal. It ran from the Mississippi River to a swamp. Behind this wall, Jackson waited for the English to attack.

13
THE BATTLE OF NEW ORLEANS

Near daybreak on January 8, 1815, Jackson saw a rocket burst over the English camp. After a while he saw the English soldiers in their red coats. The redcoats were marching forward in rows.

Jackson barked an order. The big guns boomed. Smoke filled the air. It blew away. The Englishmen were still coming on.

Jackson turned to his riflemen.

"Fire!" he yelled.

A thousand rifles cracked at once.

Most of Jackson's men were from Tennessee and Kentucky. They were hunters. And they were good shots. Again and again they fired. Every time they killed more Englishmen.

The brave redcoats kept coming. But soon they could take no more. They ran. The battle was over. Two thousand Englishmen were dead or wounded. Only eight Americans had been killed, and only 13 wounded.

Before the battle, America and England had already made peace. But Jackson did not know that. And Americans did not care. The Battle of New Orleans was America's only big land victory of the War of 1812. Old Hickory was America's hero.

Many people thought Old Hickory should be President. But he soon put a stop to such talk. He said he was for James Monroe. And in 1816 Monroe was elected President.

President Monroe asked Jackson to head the army, as secretary of war. Jackson thanked him. But he said no. The post went to John C. Calhoun of South Carolina.

Monroe's secretary of state was John Quincy Adams. He had to deal with other countries. He wanted to buy Florida. He talked it over with men from the Spanish government.

From the Hermitage, Jackson kept up with what Adams was doing. He, too, was interested in Florida.

14
FIGHTING IN FLORIDA

The Indians of Florida were called Seminoles. Some of them had lived in the state of Georgia to the north. American soldiers had chased them into Florida. But the Seminoles had gone back into Georgia. There, they had attacked American towns.

Secretary of War Calhoun sent Jackson to punish the Seminoles. But Jackson had a bigger plan. He wrote to President Monroe. He said he could take over Spanish Florida.

Monroe did not say he could do it. But Jackson was sure Monroe liked his plan. He marched into Florida.

Jackson took two forts from Spain. And he captured two Englishmen. He believed that these two men had stirred up the Seminoles against the United States. He had the two men killed. Then he left Florida.

Spain was angry about the forts. England was angry about the men. Both countries said they might go to war with the United States. Men in the American government were angry, too. In secret, Secretary of War Calhoun tried to get President Monroe to punish Jackson.

But Secretary of State Adams said Old Hickory had done well. He said Jackson had shown that Spain was too weak to rule Florida.

Spain sold Florida to the United States. And President Monroe sent Jackson there as governor. But Old Hickory did not like Florida. Soon he was back home in Tennessee.

There, friends kept asking him to run for President. At last he told them he would. First, they got him to run for senator again. He won.

In 1824 he ran for President. He ran against Adams and two other men. He got more votes than any of the others. But he did not get more votes than all the others together.

It was up to the congressmen to elect the President. They elected John Quincy Adams President and John C. Calhoun Vice President.

15
BECOMING PRESIDENT

Jackson gave up being a senator. He went home. There, he made his plans to run for President again.

Many people came to see him. One was Sam Houston. Houston was like a son to Jackson. He had fought under him in the Creek War. He had been in Congress. In 1827, he became governor of Tennessee.

Houston knew Jackson wanted Calhoun as his Vice President. He warned Jackson about him. He said Calhoun had tried to have Jackson punished for fighting in Florida.

But Calhoun said it was not true.

In 1828 Jackson ran for President again. One man ran against him. He was President John Quincy Adams.

Adams's followers put stories in the newspapers. The stories told the same lies Dickinson had told. They said Rachel was not fit to be the wife of a President.

Jackson tried to keep the stories from Rachel. But she saw them. They made her very, very sad.

The American people voted. They elected Old Hickory President and John C. Calhoun Vice President.

The Jacksons got ready to move to Washington. Then Rachel fell sick. She seemed to get better. But just before Christmas, she died.

Jackson's great love was gone. He was heartbroken. His friends were afraid he might die of sorrow.

At last he pulled himself together. He went to Washington. There, he got his new government ready.

He picked Senator Martin Van Buren of New York to be secretary of state. He let Calhoun pick men for most of the other high posts.

On March 4, 1829, the sun was shining. As Old Hickory walked to the Capitol Building, people cheered. He swore to uphold the laws of the country. Now Andrew Jackson was President of the United States.

Then he rode to the White House. A huge crowd followed him there.

16
"LET THE PEOPLE RULE"

President Jackson was giving a party in the White House. It was for the heads of his government. But the people loved Old Hickory. So they came, too.

Into the White House they came. They gobbled cake. They gulped ice cream. They guzzled orange drinks. Glasses, cups and dishes began to break. Chairs fell. A table crashed to the floor. And the President of the United States had to get out by the back door!

Many people worried about how good a President Jackson would be. They knew he liked to say, "Let the people rule." But the people had made a mess of his party. Would his government be a mess, too?

It seemed so. The top men in his government argued. Some took the side of Jackson and Secretary Van Buren. Others took the side of Vice President Calhoun.

One thing they argued about was the American tariff law. Americans who bought certain things made in other countries had to pay extra money to the government.

The extra tariff money made many things cost more in America.

Farmers needed many things from other countries. They did not like having to pay the tariff.

Calhoun's state, South Carolina, was a farming state. So Calhoun was against the tariff. He did not think the people of South Carolina should have to pay it.

If they did not pay, they would be breaking a law of the United States. Calhoun said that was all right. He said a state government could turn down a law of the United States.

But if the states did that, each would be like a little country. They would no longer be united. Their union would break up. Old Hickory knew he must answer Calhoun.

17
SIX GREAT WORDS

In April, 1830, a dinner party was held in Washington. Jackson came. So did Vice President Calhoun.

One by one, friends of Calhoun stood up and spoke. They all agreed with Calhoun. They all said that each state could do as it liked.

Jackson's turn came to talk. He stood up. He lifted his wine glass. And he looked straight at Calhoun.

"Our Union," he said firmly, "it must be preserved."

Calhoun looked pale. His hand shook. He did not want to drink to the Union. But he had to.

The President's six great words were a warning. Now Calhoun knew how Jackson felt. Jackson would never let the country break up.

Matters between the two men soon grew worse. Jackson read a letter. It was from a man who had worked with Calhoun for President Monroe. It said Calhoun had tried to have Old Hickory punished for fighting in Florida.

Sam Houston had been right about Calhoun after all.

Jackson was done with Calhoun. He worked with Van Buren instead. He took command of his government. He showed he could command in peace as well as he had in war.

In 1832 Jackson faced a big fight. It was over the United States Bank. The Bank was the biggest bank in America. It was owned by a few men. These men were rich and powerful.

A law said the Bank must go out of business in 1836. That was fine with Jackson. He did not like the Bank. He did not think a few rich men should have so much power over the American people.

But Senator Henry Clay liked the Bank. He wanted to have a new law passed. His law would give the Bank many more years to run.

The congressmen argued about Clay's law. Some were against it. But more seemed to be for it.

18

"KING ANDREW THE FIRST"

In May, 1832, men came from all over the United States to the city of Baltimore. These men belonged to the Democratic party. They met to pick a man to run for President.

The Democrats picked Jackson to run again. He had them pick Van Buren to run for Vice President.

Old Hickory would run against the man who had written the law about the Bank, Senator Henry Clay.

In Washington the congressmen voted on Clay's law. They passed it. It would be a law of the land when the President signed it.

But Jackson would not sign it. There would be no new Bank law. After 1836 the United States Bank would be finished.

Clay and his friends were angry. They said Jackson was as bad as King George III of England. They called him "King Andrew the First."

But poor men were very glad that Jackson had stopped the Bank. They voted for him. He beat Clay. He would be President four more years.

Then he faced new trouble over the tariff. The government of South Carolina took a stand against him. It said the United States could not collect tariff money in Charleston.

At once Jackson sent warships to Charleston. He told the people of South Carolina to obey the law. The state government gave in. Tariffs were collected. Jackson had won.

Jackson got the Democrats to pick Van Buren to run for President in 1836. And Van Buren was elected.

President Jackson had one big problem left. It was Texas.

Jackson's friend Sam Houston was now President of Texas. Texas had belonged to Mexico. Houston had led Americans there in a war against Mexico. They had won. They had set up a government. Houston wanted America to recognize Texas. He wanted America to say Texas was a free country, not a part of Mexico.

Jackson knew this would make Mexico angry. At first he said no. But on his last day as President he gave in. He recognized Texas.

19
THE LAST YEARS

Old Hickory went back home to the Hermitage. Over the years he had made it bigger and more beautiful.

At the Hermitage, his "family" of slaves took care of him. His adopted children came to see him. They brought their own children to see the great old man.

Important men visited him, too. President Van Buren came from Washington. Sam Houston came all the way from Texas.

Even though Jackson was not the President any more, people still wanted his help.

In 1844 the Democrats could not agree on the right man to run for President. Jackson asked them to pick James K. Polk of Tennessee. They did. In the election Polk beat Jackson's old enemy, Henry Clay.

This pleased Jackson. But other news did not. More and more people in the North were saying it was not right to own slaves. People in the South did not like this. America was dividing over slavery.

In March, 1845, Congress voted to let Texas into the Union as a state. And Florida at last became a state.

By now Jackson was 78 years old. He was sick. He wanted to see Sam Houston once more before he died.

Jackson sent for Houston. But it took many days for his letter to get to Texas. He grew weaker every day. On June 8, 1845, at six o'clock in the afternoon, he died. His slaves cried. And they sang a sad old song.

That evening Sam Houston came at last with his little boy. Crying, he fell to his knees by Jackson's bed. Then he turned to his son.

"My son," he told the boy, "try to remember that you have looked on the face of Andrew Jackson."

AFTER ANDREW JACKSON

Jackson had been right. Mexico was angry over losing Texas. War began between America and Mexico. America took all of Mexico's land from Texas to the Pacific Ocean.

To the north, America took over still more land between the Rocky Mountains and the Pacific Ocean.

As the years passed, the argument over slavery grew hotter. People in the South remembered that Calhoun had said the states could go their own ways. In 1860 South Carolina left the Union. Ten more states of the South soon left the Union, too.

Abraham Lincoln was President now. He agreed with Jackson's six great words, "Our Union, it must be preserved." He sent soldiers to fight for the Union.

After four years of war the states of the South gave up. The Union was saved. The idea that won out in the end was not Calhoun's. It was Andrew Jackson's.

Jackson had fought as a boy to help bring his country into being. He had fought as a soldier against its enemies. He had fought as a President to keep it together.

Americans can never forget what he did. They remember with thanks the name of Andrew Jackson.

THE WAY THE

FROM THE REVOLUTION

THE LOUISIANA PURCHASE

TEXAS
1845

MEXICO